POKÉMON TRAINER FILE

NAME:

AGE:

POKÉMON BUDDY:

Farshore

First published in Great Britain 2023 by Farshore
An imprint of HarperCollinsPublishers
1 London Bridge Street, London SE1 9GF
www.farshore.co.uk

HarperCollinsPublishers
Macken House, 39/40 Mayor Street Upper,
Dublin 1 D01 C9W8 Ireland

ISBN 978 0 00 853714 2
Printed and bound in UAE
1

A CIP catalogue record for this title is available from the British Library.

Parental guidance is advised for all craft and colouring activities. Always ask an adult to help
when using glue, paint and scissors. Wear protective clothing and cover surfaces to avoid staining.

Stay safe online. Farshore is not responsible for content hosted by third parties.

MIX
Paper | Supporting
responsible forestry
FSC™ C007454

This book is produced from independently certified FSC™ paper
to ensure responsible forest management.

For more information visit: www.harpercollins.co.uk/green

ANNUAL 2024

CONTENTS

TAKE ME ON A JOURNEY!

HEY TRAINER, YOUR ADVENTURE STARTS RIGHT HERE.

Join Ash and Goh on their action-packed journey through the world of Pokémon. They're ready to travel far and wide through the Galar region and beyond, whether it's to do battle or to catch as many Pokémon as they can.

ARE YOU READY TO CHALLENGE YOUR OWN SKILLS?

Check out the epic puzzles, try your luck with the games, and read the stories. When you're ready, jump in to the Pokédex A-Z to discover some awesome Pokémon data.

LET'S GO!

Ash's buddy Pikachu is with him every step of the way. **How many times can you spot this picture throughout the book?**

ANSWERS ON PAGE 68

CATCH SOME POKÉMON!

Ash and Goh are chasing Pokémon in the Galar region, but who did they catch?

LOOK CAREFULLY AT PICTURE 1, THEN CAN YOU SPOT WHICH POKÉMON ARE MISSING IN PICTURE 2?

PICTURE 1

Which Pokémon evolves from Drizzile and can shoot water from its fingertips? **Spot it in the scene.**

WRITE THE MISSING POKÉMON HERE – THEY'VE BEEN CAUGHT!

PICTURE 2

One of the Pokémon that has been caught was Goh's first partner. **Who is it?**

ANSWERS ON PAGE 68

MASTER TRAINER MAZE

Journey through the Galar region and catch as many Pokémon as you can along the way.

BE PREPARED TO BATTLE ETERNATUS BEFORE YOU REACH THE FINISH LINE!

START

WILD AREA

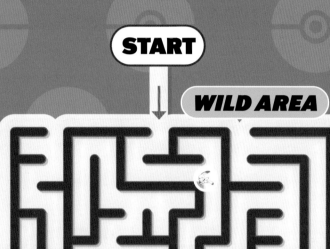

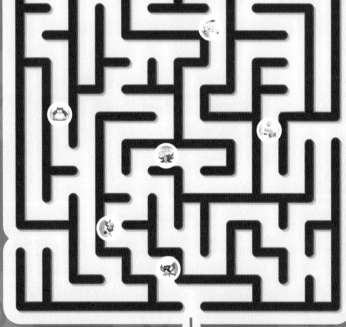

GLIMWOOD TANGLE

WYNDON

SLUMBERING WEALD

HAMMERLOCKE STADIUM

FINISH

?

Eternatus is a Legendary dual-type Pokémon, **but what are its two types?**

a. Psychic and Dragon

b. Poison and Dragon

c. Fire and Ground

ANSWERS ON PAGE 68

II

PROJECT MEW

You've been recruited as a Trainer Challenger in Project Mew! Can you complete your Trial Missions to reach chaser status?

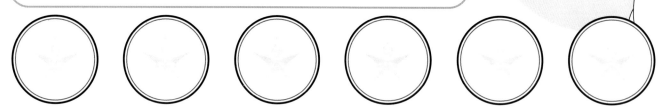

PROJECT MEW IS A SPECIAL MEW RESEARCH PROJECT.

DO YOU HAVE WHAT IT TAKES TO JOIN THE TEAM?

Colour these tokens as you complete each mission.

TRIAL MISSION 1   EARN 2 TOKENS

Your first mission is to catch a Milotic! Draw three straight lines to divide the space so that each division has only one Pokémon. **Milotic should be caught in the middle!**

TRIAL MISSION 2

EARN 3 TOKENS

Warm up your psychic energy! How many times does RALTS appear in the grid? **Don't miss any, Challenger!**

X	L	R	B	W	V	S	T	L	A	R	K	Y	P	D
H	R	A	L	T	S	C	Z	M	B	V	C	G	J	R
R	A	L	T	S	T	E	U	R	A	L	T	S	O	A
I	B	T	K	E	L	N	S	T	L	A	R	W	Q	L
E	F	S	T	L	A	R	I	O	H	E	Z	P	B	T
M	Y	D	I	U	R	A	L	T	S	R	A	L	T	S

TRIAL MISSION 3 EARN **1** TOKEN

Complete the grid art by colouring the dotted squares with matching colours. **Poké Ball, go!**

DID YOU COMPLETE YOUR MISSIONS? WAY TO GO, CHASER!

ANSWERS ON PAGE 68

THE HUNT FOR MEW

Help Goh by making Mew visible. Use colouring pencils to shade the correct sections and make this Mythical Pokémon stand out!

ANSWER ON PAGE 68

ELECTRIC WORDSEARCH

Charge up, Trainer!
Can you find these Electric-type Pokémon hiding in the grid?

JOLTEON	CHARJABUG	DRACOZOLT	GALVANTULA	TOXTRICITY
JOLTIK	MORPEKO	PICHU	PIKACHU	PINCURCHIN
	RAICHU	TOXEL	BOLTUND	

J J A J O R Z G J C ⚡ I I K J
O E T I G E ⚡ A T D U R O I M
N ⚡ A Y N P J L O H L R K T E
G Z J H ⚡ M Z V X R U Y E L ⚡
R E T K Z A H A T H K M P U G
P A J O L Y ⚡ N R M ⚡ M R J T
V I I O X J N T I J J A O G L
G ⚡ N C V E X U C O P H M U O
N B Y C H D L L I L I H I B Z
N E O E U U ⚡ A T T K G R A O
H E N L R R Z R Y E A I ⚡ J C
O ⚡ J G T D C V ⚡ O C R U R A
G K I M U U P H H N H C A A R
P I C H U B N V I R U A D H D
H K B U M H O D P N C O X C C
I B ⚡ K E ⚡ N S ⚡ L A R W ⚡ L
E F S T L A R I O H E ⚡ P B T
H ⚡ A J O L T I K B V C G J R

CAN YOU SPOT PROFESSOR CERISE'S ELECTRIC-TYPE PET SOMEWHERE IN THE WORDSEARCH?

A PINCH OF THIS, A PINCH OF THAT

STORY

Join Ash and Goh on an incredible fossil-finding trip to the Galar region!

Ash and Goh were on a video call at the Cerise Laboratory when Professor Cerise arrived with his daughter, Chloe.
The man on the screen was the director of the Museum of Science – he had an adventure for them.
"We're investigating fossils!" exclaimed Goh.
"And I know where," said Ash. "The Wild Area!"
"That's correct," said the director. "I heard a rumour that one can obtain extremely rare fossils in the Galar region, so I'd like you to go and investigate precisely what kinds of fossils they are."

Ash and Pikachu, Goh and Cinderace, and Chloe and her Pokémon companion Eevee were all excited about the trip. Soon they were on the plane to the Wild Area. Out of the plane window, Chloe and Eevee were amazed to see the beautiful Galar region appear on the horizon.

The gang arrived in the Wild Area and were amazed to see so many different Pokémon living there.
Suddenly, a huge Pokémon appeared and Eevee squealed in terror. Chloe scanned it on her Rotom Phone: *Boldore, the Ore Pokémon, a Rock-type. It uses sound waves to search the area around it. When angry it gives chase without changing the direction it's facing.*

The Boldore started to attack Eevee, but Cinderace managed to knock Boldore to the ground. Ash quickly caught it with his Poké Ball. "Thank you so much," said Chloe, holding on tight to Eevee.

The gang soon found a team of fossil-hunters picking away at rocks.
"So this is where it all happens," said Goh. They were just about to start hunting when they heard: "Mudsdale, Double Kick!" and a huge thud as a Mudsdale Pokémon bashed through some rocks.

It turned out Mudsdale belonged to a researcher called Bray Zenn. Ash told Bray they were there to look for rare fossils, and Bray showed them where to start. "Dig around," said Bray. "If you keep at it, you should be able to find the entire structures." Just then, another researcher showed up. Her name was Cara Liss and she was rather careless. She had forgotten to bring her pickaxe.

Gradually they all collected many fossilised bones. They laid them out on the ground and tried to work out how the bones fit together.

Cara took two sets of bones and pulled them together. She had a theory that long ago this area was under the sea, so this Pokémon would've needed limbs that made it easy to travel in water, and its head would have had to face upwards to help it eat. "I'll name it Arctovish!"

"Now my turn," said Bray Zenn. He took another two sets of fossils and explained his theory, that long ago this area was a plain with nothing but stunted trees. Flying Pokémon found that running was better than flying, so they developed stronger legs. He named his Pokémon Dracozolt!

Bray Zenn and Cara Liss packed up the fossils in separate boxes, but they got confused about which fossils were in which box.

In the end, Bray Zenn gave up trying to sort them out. "Let's take the next step," he said.

"Ta-da!" said Cara. "Presenting the Fossil Restorer Machine! It takes a fossil that's in pieces and restores it to its original state. Isn't it great?"

Cara turned the machine on and it zapped the boxes of fossils.

Eventually, the Fossil Restorer Machine beeped – it was finished!
They pressed the extraction button and out zapped two very strange looking Pokémon!
The machine had muddled up Bray and Cara's two theories. Bray named his new
Pokémon Arctozolt, and Cara called hers Dracovish.

Just then, Dracovish started chasing Ash!
Pikachu tried to stop Dracovish, but it didn't
work. Dracovish shot a powerful stream of
water out of its mouth, which hit Arctozolt
in the face! This made Arctozolt angry – it
started to breathe out sheets of ice. The
Fossil Pokémon were out of control!

Dracovish, Ash and Pikachu all slid on a sheet of Arctozolt's ice, and Ash and Pikachu ended up clinging onto the Fossil Pokémon's back. Dracovish started running very fast.

"Can't you just stop running?!" yelled Ash, but it wouldn't listen. Before long, Dracovish dived into a deep lake. It turned out it just wanted to swim – it was happy now!

Meanwhile, Goh needed to protect Chloe and Eevee from an angry Arctozolt. He summoned Boldore, who he'd collected earlier that day. The two Pokémon faced off, and Arctozolt quickly calmed down when he realised he couldn't win.

Dracovish, Ash and Pikachu reappeared, and everyone was pleased that the Fossil Pokémon were happy and calm now!

The researchers Bray and Cara had a question for the team. "Would you mind looking after the new Fossil Pokémon for us?" So Ash and Goh each got a new Pokémon registered to their Pokédex: Arctozolt and Dracovish! "We caught 'em!" they yelled.

ASH AND GOH HAVE SOME BRAND-NEW FOSSIL POKÉMON FRIENDS, AND CHLOE DISCOVERED THE FUN OF GOING ON AN ADVENTURE WITH HER POKÉMON PARTNER. THERE ARE SO MANY NEW PEOPLE AND POKÉMON TO MEET, AS THE JOURNEY CONTINUES...

DNA MIX-UP!

Imagine if these Pokémon had their DNA mixed up – what two new Pokémon might they make, and what could you name them?

WHEN DRACOZOLT AND ARCTOVISH WERE MIXED UP, RESEARCHERS CREATED DRACOVISH AND ARCTOZOLT! WHAT WILL YOUR MEGA MIX-UPS LOOK LIKE?

RILLABOOM   CINDERACE

OBSTAGOON   SILICOBRA

MAP THOSE MOVES!

Hey Trainer, some awesome Pokémon have been located across the Galar region. **Can you identify them and then find their coordinates on the map?**

To locate their coordinates, find the matching square in the grid, then note its number and letter. **For example, this is 3B.**

1. This Pokémon is made up of six individuals, but only one is in charge. Who is it?

2. Which Pokémon has psychic power stored in the fur above its hooves?

3. Which Fox Pokémon survives by stealing food from others?

4. Which Galarian Ground- and Steel-type Pokémon lives in the mud?

5. When this hungry Pokémon is finished eating, it goes promptly to sleep! Who is it?

6. Which Pokémon's curly fleece is such a strong cushion it could survive a fall off a cliff?

	A	B	C	D	E	F	G	H
1								
2								
3								
4								
5								
6								
7								
8								
9								
10								
11								
12								
13								
14								
15								
16								
17								
18								
19								
20								
21								

ANSWERS ON PAGE 69

WORLD CORONATION SERIES

DO YOU HAVE WHAT IT TAKES TO BE THE WCS CHAMPION?

Write in pencil, then you can erase and play again!

NORMAL CLASS

 CENTISKORCH   CLOBBOPUS

BATTLE 1

 DREDNAW  INTELEON

BATTLE 2

 GALARIAN FARFETCH'D   OBSTAGOON

BATTLE 3

 GROOKEY  CINDERACE

BATTLE 4

GREAT CLASS

_____

_____

BATTLE 9

_____

_____

BATTLE 10

ULTRA CLASS

_____

_____

BATTLE 13

MASTER CLASS

_____

BATTLE 15

HOW TO PLAY:

YOU'LL NEED:

2 – 4 players

A coin

1. Take turns to choose your Pokémon in Normal Class.
   The youngest player goes first. Add your initial next to your choices.
2. Work through the battles in order, with two players facing off each time.
   One player calls heads or tails, then tosses the coin to find the winner.
3. Whoever wins writes the name of their victorious Pokémon in the box below.
4. Keep playing through Great Class and Ultra Class, until you get to Master Class and the final.
5. To find the World Coronation Series champ, play a best-of-three coin toss!

NORMAL CLASS

COALOSSAL MORPEKO DRAGAPULT CORVIKNIGHT DURALUDON FALINKS GRIMMSNARL DRACOVISH

BATTLE **5** BATTLE **6** BATTLE **7** BATTLE **8**

GREAT CLASS

BATTLE **11** BATTLE **12**

ULTRA CLASS

BATTLE **14**

MASTER CLASS

BATTLE **15**

CHAMP!

FANTASTIC FLYERS

How many Flying-type Pokémon can you catch?

NAME EACH ONE TO REGISTER THEM TO YOUR POKÉDEX!

ADD THE NAMES HERE:

_____   _____   _____

_____   _____

_____   _____   _____

 What Legendary Fire- and Flying-type Pokémon did Ash and Goh look for in the Johto region?

_____

ANSWERS ON PAGE 69

POKÉDEX A-Z

Ash and Goh are having an awesome time on their journey around the different regions. They're making lots of incredible discoveries and reporting their findings to Professor Cerise in Vermilion City.

RESEARCH THE NEXT FEW PAGES FOR DATA ON SOME POKÉMON FROM GALAR, KALOS AND BEYOND. ARE YOU DRAWN TO THE ELECTRIC-, FIRE- OR FIGHTING-TYPE POKÉMON? WHAT LEGENDARY AND MYTHICAL POKÉMON WILL YOU SPOT?

Circle the Pokémon you'd most love to catch. Poké Ball, go!

When it trusts a Trainer, it will treat them to berries it's decorated with cream.

ALCREMIE

FAIRY

| 0.3 m | 0.5 kg |

Its body is covered in sweet nectar, and the skin on its back is especially yummy. Children used to have it as a snack.

APPLETUN

GRASS · DRAGON

| 0.4 m | 13.0 kg |

It spends its entire life inside an apple. It hides from its natural enemies, bird Pokémon, by pretending it's just an apple and nothing more.

APPLIN

GRASS · DRAGON

| 0.2 m | 0.5 kg |

The sight of it running over 9,978 km in a single day and night has captivated many people.

ARCANINE

FIRE

| 1.9 m | 155.0 kg |

Though it's able to capture prey by freezing its surroundings, it has trouble eating the prey afterwards because its mouth is on top of its head.

ARCTOVISH

WATER · ICE

| 2.0 m | 175.0 kg |

This Pokémon lived on prehistoric seashores and was able to preserve food with the ice on its body. It went extinct because it moved so slowly.

ARCTOZOLT

ELECTRIC · ICE

| 2.3 m | 150.0 kg |

If it sees any movement around it, this Pokémon charges for it straight away, leading with its sharply pointed jaw. It's very proud of that jaw.

ARROKUDA

WATER

| 0.5 m | 1.0 kg |

This Pokémon has a jaw that's as sharp as a spear and as strong as steel. Apparently Barraskewda's flesh is surprisingly tasty, too.

BARRASKEWDA

GRASS · DRAGON

| 1.3 m | 30.0 kg |

Blastoise has waterspouts that protrude from its shell. The waterspouts are very accurate. They can shoot bullets of water with enough accuracy to strike empty cans from a distance of over 49 m.

BLASTOISE

WATER

| 1.6 m | 85.5 kg |

A constant collector of information, this Pokémon is very smart. Very strong is what it isn't.

BLIPBUG

BUG

| 0.4 m | 8.0 kg |

This Pokémon generates electricity and channels it into its legs to keep them going strong. Boltund can run non-stop for three full days.

BOLTUND

ELECTRIC

| 1.0 m | 34.0 kg |

Known for its bravery and pride, this majestic Pokémon is often seen as a motif for various kinds of emblems.

BRAVIARY

FLYING

| 1.5 m | 41.0 kg |

Bulbasaur can be seen napping in bright sunlight. There is a seed on its back. By soaking up the sun's rays, the seed grows progressively larger.

BULBASAUR

GRASS

| 0.7 m | 6.9 kg |

In battle, it flaps its wings at great speed to release highly toxic dust into the air.

BUTTERFREE

BUG · FLYING

| 1.1 m | 32.0 kg |

It forms coal inside its body. Coal dropped by this Pokémon once helped fuel the lives of people in the Galar region.

CARKOL

ROCK · FIRE

| 1.1 m | 78.0 kg |

While its burning body is already dangerous on its own, this excessively hostile Pokémon also has large and very sharp fangs.

CENTISKORCH

FIRE · BUG

| 3.0 m | 120.0 kg |

It spits fire that is hot enough to melt boulders. It may cause forest fires by blowing flames.

CHARIZARD

FIRE · FLYING

| 1.7 m | 90.5 kg |

While its durable shell protects it from attacks, Charjabug strikes at enemies with jolts of electricity discharged from the tips of its jaws.

CHARJABUG

BUG · ELECTRIC

| 0.5 m | 10.5 kg |

It has a preference for hot things. When it rains, steam is said to spout from the tip of its tail.

CHARMANDER

FIRE

| 0.6 m | 8.5 kg |

It has a barbaric nature. In battle, it whips its fiery tail around and slashes away with sharp claws.

CHARMELEON

FIRE

| 1.1 m | 19.0 kg |

It starts off battles by attacking with its rock-hard horn, but as soon as the opponent flinches, this Pokémon bites down and never lets go.

CHEWTLE

WATER

| 0.3 m | 8.5 kg |

It's skilled at both offence and defence, and it gets pumped up when cheered on. But if it starts showboating, it could put itself in a tough spot.

CINDERACE

FIRE

| 1.4 m | 33.0 kg |

Its tentacles tear off easily, but it isn't alarmed when that happens – it knows they'll grow back. It's about as smart as a three-year-old.

CLOBBOPUS

FIGHTING

| 0.6 m | 4.0 kg |

While it's engaged in battle, its mountain of coal will burn bright red, sending off sparks that scorch the surrounding area.

COALOSSAL

ROCK · FIRE

| 2.8 m | 310.5 kg |

These Pokémon live in herds. Their trunks have incredible grip strength, strong enough to crush giant rocks into powder.

COPPERAJAH

STEEL

| 3.0 m | 650.0 kg |

Sudden climate change wiped out this ancient kind of Corsola. This Pokémon absorbs others' life-force through its branches.

GALARIAN CORSOLA

GHOST

| 0.6 m | 0.5 kg |

With their great intellect and flying skills, these Pokémon very successfully act as the Galar region's airborne taxi service.

CORVIKNIGHT

FLYING · STEEL

| 2.2 m | 75.0 kg |

Smart enough to use tools in battle, these Pokémon have been seen picking up rocks and flinging them or using ropes to wrap up enemies.

CORVISQUIRE

FLYING

| 0.8 m | 16.0 kg |

This hungry Pokémon swallows Arrokuda whole. Occasionally, it makes a mistake and tries to swallow a Pokémon other than its preferred prey.

CRAMORANT

FLYING · WATER

| 0.8 m | 18.0 kg |

If a job requires serious strength, this Pokémon will excel at it. Its copper body tarnishes in the rain, turning a vibrant green colour.

CUFANT

STEEL

| 1.2 m | 100.0 kg |

Be cautious of the ectoplasmic body surrounding its soul. You'll become stiff as stone if you touch it.

CURSOLA

GHOST

| 1.0 m | 0.4 kg |

On days when blizzards blow through, it comes down to where people live. It stashes food in the snowball on its head, taking it home for later.

GALARIAN DARMANITAN

ICE

| 1.7 m | 120.0 kg |

It lived in snowy areas for so long that its fire sac cooled off and atrophied. It now has an organ that generates cold instead.

GALARIAN DARUMAKA

ICE

| 0.7 m | 40.0 kg |

It barely moves, but it's still alive. Hiding in its shell without food or water seems to have awakened its psychic powers.

DOTTLER

BUG · PSYCHIC

| 0.4 m | 19.5 kg |

Its mighty legs are capable of running at speeds exceeding 40 mph, but this Pokémon can't breathe unless it's underwater.

DRACOVISH

WATER · DRAGON

| 2.3 m | 215.0 kg |

The powerful muscles in its tail generate its electricity. Compared to its lower body, its upper half is entirely too small.

DRACOZOLT

ELECTRIC · DRAGON

| 1.8 m | 190.0 kg |

When it isn't battling, it keeps Dreepy in the holes on its horns. Once a fight starts, it launches the Dreepy like supersonic missiles.

DRAGAPULT

DRAGON · GHOST

| 3.0 m | 50.0 kg |

It's capable of flying faster than 120 mph. It battles alongside Dreepy and dotes on them until they successfully evolve.

DRAKLOAK

DRAGON · GHOST

| 1.4 m | 11.0 kg |

With jaws that can shear through steel rods, this highly aggressive Pokémon chomps down on its unfortunate prey.

DREDNAW

WATER · ROCK

| 1.0 m | 115.5 kg |

After being reborn as a ghost Pokémon, Dreepy wanders the areas it used to inhabit back when it was alive in prehistoric seas.

DREEPY

DRAGON · GHOST

| 0.5 m | 2.0 kg |

Highly intelligent, but also very lazy, it keeps enemies out of its territory by laying traps everywhere.

DRIZZILE

WATER

| 0.7 m | 11.5 kg |

Weave a carpet from its springy wool, and you end up with something closer to a trampoline. You'll start to bounce the moment you set foot on it.

DUBWOOL

NORMAL

| 1.3 m | 43.0 kg |

The special metal that composes its body is very light, so this Pokémon has considerable agility. It lives in caves because it dislikes the rain.

DURALUDON

STEEL · DRAGON

| 1.8 m | 40.0 kg |

Thanks to its unstable genetic make-up, this special Pokémon conceals many different possible Evolutions.

EEVEE

NORMAL

| 0.3 m | 6.5 kg |

This Pokémon keeps its heat-sensitive head cool with ice. It fishes for its food, dangling its single hair into the sea to lure in prey.

EISCUE

ICE

| 1.4 m | 89.0 kg |

The cotton on the head of this Pokémon can be spun into a glossy, gorgeous yarn – a Galar-regional speciality.

ELDEGOSS

GRASS

| 0.5 m | 2.5 kg |

It unleashes psychic power from the orb on its forehead. When its power is exhausted, the orb grows dull and dark.

ESPEON

PSYCHIC

| 0.9 m | 26.5 kg |

There's enough psychic power in Espurr to send a wrestler flying, but because this power can't be controlled, Espurr finds it troublesome.

ESPURR

PSYCHIC

| 0.3 m | 3.5 kg |

The core on its chest absorbs energy emanating from the lands of the Galar region. This energy is what allows Eternatus to stay active.

ETERNATUS

POISON · DRAGON

| 20.0 m | 950.0 kg |

The six of them work together as one Pokémon. Teamwork is also their battle strategy, and they constantly change their formation as they fight.

FALINKS

FIGHTING

| 3.0 m | 62.0 kg |

The Farfetch'd of the Galar region are brave warriors, and they wield thick, tough leeks in battle.

GALARIAN FARFETCH'D

FIGHTING

| 0.8 m | 42.0 kg |

It is a shabby and ugly Pokémon. However, it is very hardy and can survive on little water.

FEEBAS

WATER

| 0.6 m | 7.4 kg |

It flies on wings of apple skin and spits a powerful acid. It can also change its shape into that of an apple.

FLAPPLE

GRASS · DRAGON

| 0.3 m | 1.0 kg |

It stores some of the air it inhales in its internal flame pouch, which heats it to almost 150 °C .

FLAREON

FIRE

| 0.9 m | 25.0 kg |

It shows no mercy to any who desecrate fields and mountains. It will fly around on its icy wings, causing a blizzard to chase offenders away.

FROSMOTH

ICE · BUG

| 1.3 m | 42.0 kg |

Sharply attuned to others' wishes for help, this Pokémon seeks out those in need and aids them in battle.

GALLADE

PSYCHIC · FIGHTING

| 1.6 m | 52.0 kg |

With its gas-like body, it can sneak into any place it desires. However, it can be blown away by wind.

GASTLY

GHOST · POISON

| 1.3 m | 0.1 kg |

On the night of a full moon, if shadows move on their own and laugh, it must be Gengar's doing.

GENGAR

GHOST · POISON

| 1.5 m | 40.5 kg |

Any who become captivated by the beauty of the snowfall that Glaceon creates will be frozen before they know it.

GLACEON

ICE

| 0.8 m | 25.9 kg |

It anchors itself in the ground with its single leg, then basks in the sun. After absorbing enough sunlight, its petals spread as it blooms brilliantly.

GOSSIFLEUR

GRASS

| 0.4 m | 2.2 kg |

A body made up of nothing but muscle makes the grappling moves this Pokémon performs with its tentacles tremendously powerful.

GRAPPLOCT

FIGHTING

| 1.6 m | 39.0 kg |

Common throughout the Galar region, this Pokémon has strong teeth and can chew through the toughest of berry shells.

GREEDENT

NORMAL

| 0.6 m | 6.0 kg |

It appears and vanishes with a ninja's grace. It toys with its enemies using swift movements, while slicing them with throwing stars of sharpest water.

GRENINJA

WATER · DARK

| 1.5 m | 40.0 kg |

With the hair wrapped around its body helping to enhance its muscles, this Pokémon can overwhelm even Machamp.

GRIMMSNARL

DARK · FAIRY

| 1.5 m | 61.0 kg |

It attacks with rapid beats of its stick. As it strikes with amazing speed, it gets more and more pumped.

GROOKEY

GRASS

| 0.3 m | 5.0 kg |

Extremely loyal, it will fearlessly bark at any opponent to protect its own Trainer from harm.

GROWLITHE

FIRE

| 0.7 m | 19.0 kg |

Once it begins to rampage, a Gyarados will burn everything down, even in a harsh storm.

GYARADOS

WATER · FLYING

| 6.5 m | 235.0 kg |

If this Pokémon senses a strong emotion, it will run away as fast as it can. It prefers areas without people.

HATENNA

PSYCHIC

| 0.4 m | 3.4 kg |

If you're too loud around it, you risk being torn apart by the claws on its tentacle. This Pokémon is also known as the Forest Witch.

HATTERENE

PSYCHIC · FAIRY

| 2.1 m | 5.1 kg |

Using the braids on its head, it pummels foes to get them to quiet down. One blow from those braids would knock out a professional boxer.

HATTREM

PSYCHIC

| 0.6 m | 4.8 kg |

If you get the feeling of being watched in darkness when nobody is around, Haunter is there.

HAUNTER

GHOST · POISON

| 1.6 m | 0.1 kg |

It always strikes a pose before going for its finishing move. Sometimes opponents take advantage of that time to counter-attack.

HAWLUCHA

FIGHTING · FLYING

| 0.8 m | 21.5 kg |

It sneaks into people's homes, stealing things and feasting on the negative energy of the frustrated occupants.

IMPIDIMP

DARK · FAIRY

| 0.4 m | 5.5 kg |

Through its horns, it can pick up on the emotions of creatures around it. Positive emotions are the source of its strength.

INDEEDEE

PSYCHIC · NORMAL

| 0.9 m | 28.0 kg |

It has many hidden capabilities, such as fingertips that can shoot water and a membrane on its back that it can use to glide through the air.

INTELEON

WATER

| 1.9 m | 45.2 kg |

There is a bud on this Pokémon's back. To support its weight, Ivysaur's legs and trunk grow thick and strong. If it starts spending more time lying in the sunlight, it's a sign that the bud will bloom into a large flower soon.

IVYSAUR

GRASS · POISON

| 1.0 m | 13.0 kg |

If it is angered or startled, the fur all over its body bristles like sharp needles that pierce foes.

JOLTEON

ELECTRIC

| 0.8 m | 24.5 kg |

Joltik latch on to other Pokémon and suck out static electricity. They're often found sticking to Yamper's hindquarters.

JOLTIK

BUG · ELECTRIC

| 0.1 m | 0.6 kg |

LEGENDARY

Kubfu trains hard to perfect its moves. The moves it masters will determine which form it takes when it evolves.

KUBFU

FIGHTING

| 0.6 m | 12.0 kg |

Galarians favour the distinctive aroma that drifts from this Pokémon's leaves. There's a popular perfume made using that scent.

LEAFEON

GRASS

| 1.0 m | 25.5 kg |

It uses its long tongue to taunt opponents. Once the opposition is enraged, this Pokémon hurls itself at the opponent, tackling them forcefully.

GALARIAN LINOONE

DARK · NORMAL

| 0.5 m | 32.5 kg |

It can tell what people are thinking. Only Trainers who have justice in their hearts can earn this Pokémon's trust.

LUCARIO

FIGHTING · STEEL

| 1.2 m | 54.0 kg |

Revealing the eyelike patterns on the insides of its ears will unleash its psychic powers. It normally keeps the patterns hidden, however.

MEOWSTIC

PSYCHIC

| 0.6 m | 8.5 kg |

It washes its face regularly to keep the coin on its forehead spotless. It doesn't get along with Galarian Meowth.

MEOWTH

NORMAL

| 0.4 m | 4.2 kg |

Living with a savage, seafaring people has toughened this Pokémon's body so much that parts of it have turned to iron.

GALARIAN MEOWTH

STEEL

| 0.4 m | 7.5 kg |

MYTHICAL

Mew is said to possess the genetic composition of all Pokémon. It is capable of making itself invisible at will, so it entirely avoids notice even if it approaches people.

MEW

PSYCHIC

| 0.4 m | 4.0 kg |

LEGENDARY

Mewtwo is a Pokémon that was created by genetic manipulation. However, even though the scientific power of humans created this Pokémon's body, they failed to endow Mewtwo with a compassionate heart.

MEWTWO

PSYCHIC

| 2.0 m | 122.0 kg |

This Pokémon was born from sweet-smelling particles in the air. Its body is made of cream.

MILCERY

FAIRY

| 0.2 m | 0.3 kg |

Milotic has provided inspiration to many artists.
It has even been referred to as the most beautiful Pokémon of all.

MILOTIC

WATER

| 6.2 m | 162.0 kg |

With sly cunning, it tries to lure people into the woods. Some believe it to have the power to make crops grow.

MORGREM

DARK · FAIRY

| 0.8 m | 12.5 kg |

As it eats the seeds stored up in its pocket-like pouches, this Pokémon is not just satisfying its constant hunger. It's also generating electricity.

MORPEKO

ELECTRIC · DARK

| 0.3 m | 3.0 kg |

It can radiate chilliness from the bottoms of its feet.
It'll spend the whole day tap-dancing on a frozen floor.

GALARIAN MR. MIME

ICE · PSYCHIC

| 1.4 m | 56.8 kg |

Its amusing movements make it very popular. It releases its psychic power from the pattern on its belly.

MR. RIME

ICE · PSYCHIC

| 1.5 m | 58.2 kg |

Aided by the soft pads on its feet, it silently raids the food stores of other Pokémon. It survives off its ill-gotten gains.

NICKIT

DARK

| 0.6 m | 8.9 kg |

It evolved after experiencing numerous fights. While crossing its arms, it lets out a shout that would make any opponent flinch.

OBSTAGOON

DARK · NORMAL

| 1.6 m | 46.0 kg |

It's famous for its high level of intelligence, and the large size of its brain is proof that it also possesses immense psychic power.

ORBEETLE

BUG · PSYCHIC

| 0.4 m | 40.8 kg |

Wanting to make sure it's taken seriously, Pancham's always giving others a glare. But if it's not focusing, it ends up smiling.

PANCHAM

FIGHTING

| 0.6 m | 8.0 kg |

What appears to be an iron helmet is actually hardened hair. This Pokémon lives for the thrill of battle.

PERRSERKER

STEEL

| 0.8 m | 28.0 kg |

Despite its small size, it can zap even adult humans. However, if it does so, it also surprises itself.

PICHU

ELECTRIC

| 0.3 m | 2.0 kg |

When Pikachu meet, they'll touch their tails together and exchange electricity through them as a form of greeting.

PIKACHU

ELECTRIC

| 0.4 m | 6.0 kg |

It feeds on seaweed, using its teeth to scrape it off rocks. Electric current flows from the tips of its spines.

PINCURCHIN

ELECTRIC

| 0.3 m | 1.0 kg |

Leaving leftover black tea unattended is asking for this Pokémon to come along and pour itself into it, turning the tea into a new Polteageist.

POLTEAGEIST

GHOST

| 0.2 m | 0.4 kg |

Its small horn hides a healing power. With a few rubs from this Pokémon's horn, any slight wound you have will be healed.

GALARIAN PONYTA

PSYCHIC

| 1.0 m | 30.0 kg |

If it uses its mysterious power, Psyduck can't remember having done so. It apparently can't form a memory of such an event because it goes into an altered state that is much like deep sleep.

PSYDUCK

PSYCHIC

| 0.4 m | 4.0 kg |

Its thick and fluffy fur protects it from the cold and enables it to use hotter fire moves.

RABOOT

FIRE

| 0.6 m | 9.0 kg |

Its long tail serves as a ground to protect itself from its own high-voltage power.

RAICHU

ELECTRIC

| 0.8 m | 30.0 kg |

Brave and prideful, this Pokémon dashes airily through the forest, its steps aided by the psychic power stored in the fur on its fetlocks.

GALARIAN RAPIDASH

PSYCHIC · FAIRY

| 1.7 m | 80.0 kg |

The one with the best drumming techniques becomes the boss of the troop. It has a gentle disposition and values harmony among its group.

RILLABOOM

GRASS

| 2.1 m | 90.0 kg |

It's exceedingly energetic, with enough stamina to keep running all through the night. Taking it for walks can be a challenging experience.

RIOLU

FIGHTING

| 0.7 m | 20.2 kg |

Most of its body has the same composition as coal. Fittingly, this Pokémon was first discovered in coal mines about 400 years ago.

ROLYCOLY

ROCK

| 0.3 m | 12.0 kg |

It will bravely challenge any opponent, no matter how powerful. This Pokémon benefits from every battle – even a defeat increases its strength a bit.

ROOKIDEE

FLYING

| 0.2 m | 1.8 kg |

A powerful curse was woven into an ancient painting. After absorbing the spirit of a Yamask, the painting began to move.

RUNERIGUS

GROUND · GHOST

| 1.6 m | 66.6 kg |

Its unique style of coiling allows it to blast sand out of its sand sac more efficiently.

SANDACONDA

GROUND

| 3.8 m | 65.5 kg |

A warm-up of running around gets fire energy coursing through this Pokémon's body. Once that happens, it's ready to fight at full power.

SCORBUNNY

FIRE

| 0.3 m | 4.5 kg |

It spews sand from its nostrils. While the enemy is blinded, it burrows into the ground to hide.

SILICOBRA

GROUND

| 2.2 m | 7.6 kg |

This Pokémon is said to have been born when a lonely spirit possessed a cold, leftover cup of tea.

SINISTEA

GHOST

| 0.1 m | 0.2 kg |

Only Farfetch'd that have survived many battles can attain this evolution. When this Pokémon's leek withers, it will retire from combat.

SIRFETCH'D

FIGHTING

| 0.8 m | 117.0 kg |

It stores flammable gas in its body and uses it to generate heat. The yellow sections on its belly get particularly hot.

SIZZLIPEDE

FIRE · BUG

| 0.7 m | 1.0 kg |

Found throughout the Galar region, this Pokémon becomes uneasy if its cheeks are ever completely empty of berries.

SKWOVET

NORMAL

| 0.3 m | 2.5 kg |

It eats snow that has accumulated on the ground. It prefers soft, freshly fallen snow, so it will eat its way up a mountain, aiming for the peak.

SNOM

ICE · BUG

| 0.3 m | 3.8 kg |

This Pokémon's stomach is so strong, even eating mouldy or rotten food will not affect it.

SNORLAX

NORMAL

| 2.1 m | 460.0 kg |

When scared, this Pokémon cries. Its tears pack the chemical punch of 100 onions, and attackers won't be able to resist weeping.

SOBBLE

WATER

| 0.3 m | 4.0 kg |

Squirtle's shell is not merely used for protection. The shell's rounded shape and the grooves on its surface help minimize resistance in water, enabling this Pokémon to swim at high speeds.

SQUIRTLE

WATER

| 0.5 m | 9.0 kg |

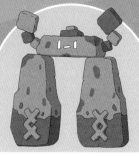

It stands in grasslands, watching the sun's descent from zenith to horizon. This Pokémon has a talent for delivering dynamic kicks.

STONJOURNER

ROCK

| 2.5 m | 520.0 kg |

Living in mud with a high iron content has given it a strong steel body.

GALARIAN STUNFISK

GROUND · STEEL

| 0.7 m | 20.5 kg |

There's a Galarian fairy tale that describes a beautiful Sylveon vanquishing a dreadful dragon Pokémon.

SYLVEON

FAIRY

| 1.0 m | 23.5 kg |

It secretly marks potential targets with a scent. By following the scent, it stalks its targets and steals from them when they least expect it.

THIEVUL

DARK

| 1.2 m | 19.9 kg |

The faster a Thwackey can beat out a rhythm with its two sticks, the more respect it wins from its peers.

THWACKEY

GRASS

| 0.7 m | 14.0 kg |

It stores poison in an internal poison sac and secretes that poison through its skin. If you touch this Pokémon, a tingling sensation follows.

TOXEL

ELECTRIC · POISON

| 0.4 m | 11.0 kg |

Capable of generating 15,000 volts of electricity, this Pokémon looks down on all that would challenge it.

TOXTRICITY

ELECTRIC · POISON

| 1.6 m | 40.0 kg |

On the night of a full moon, or when it gets excited, the ring patterns on its body glow yellow.

UMBREON

DARK

| 1.0 m | 27.0 kg |

LEGENDARY

This form of Urshifu is a strong believer in the one-hit KO. Its strategy is to leap in close to foes and land a devastating blow with a hardened fist.

URSHIFU

FIGHTING · DARK

| 1.9 m | 105.0 kg |

When Vaporeon's fins begin to vibrate, it is a sign that rain will come within a few hours.

VAPOREON

WATER

| 1.0 m | 29.0 kg |

There is a large flower on Venusaur's back. The flower is said to take on vivid colours if it gets plenty of nutrition and sunlight. The flower's aroma soothes the emotions of people.

VENUSAUR

GRASS · POISON

| 2.0 m | 100.0 kg |

Its tail is large and covered with a rich, thick fur. The tail becomes increasingly deeper in colour as Wartortle ages. The scratches on its shell are evidence of this Pokémon's toughness as a battler.

WARTORTLE

WATER

| 1.0 m | 22.5 kg |

This Pokémon consumes particles that contaminate the air. Instead of leaving droppings, it expels clean air.

GALARIAN WEEZING

POISON · FAIRY

| 1.1 m | 34.0 kg |

It hates light and shock. If attacked, it inflates its body to pump up its counterstrike.

WOBBUFFET

PSYCHIC

| 1.3 m | 28.5 kg |

Its curly fleece is such an effective cushion that this Pokémon could fall off a cliff and stand right back up at the bottom, unharmed.

WOOLOO

NORMAL

| 0.6 m | 6.0 kg |

It's said that this Pokémon was formed when an ancient clay tablet was drawn to a vengeful spirit.

GALARIAN YAMASK

GROUND · GHOST

| 0.5 m | 1.5 kg |

This Pokémon is very popular as a herding dog in the Galar region. As it runs, it generates electricity from the base of its tail.

YAMPER

ELECTRIC

| 0.3 m | 13.5 kg |

LEGENDARY

Able to cut down anything with a single strike, it became known as the Fairy King's Sword, and it inspired awe in friend and foe alike.

ZACIAN

FAIRY · STEEL

| 2.8 m | 355.0 kg |

LEGENDARY

Its ability to deflect any attack led to it being known as the Fighting Master's Shield. It was feared and respected by all.

ZAMAZENTA

FIGHTING · STEEL

| 2.9 m | 785.0 kg |

MYTHICAL

Within dense forests, this Pokémon lives in a pack with others of its kind. It's incredibly aggressive, and the other Pokémon of the forest fear it.

ZARUDE

DARK · GRASS

| 1.8 m | 70.0 kg |

Thought to be the oldest form of Zigzagoon, it moves in zigzags and wreaks havoc upon its surroundings.

GALARIAN ZIGZAGOON

DARK · NORMAL

| 0.4 m | 17.5 kg |

LIFE IN THE LAB

Professor Cerise has asked you to be a research assistant in The Cerise Laboratory!

COMPLETE THE ACTIVITIES BELOW TO HELP HIM WITH HIS LATEST POKÉMON STUDIES.

UNDER THE MICROSCOPE

Can you identify the Pokémon by studying their close-ups?

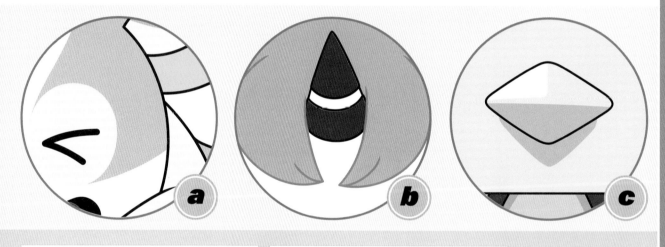

a

a _____   b _____

c _____   d _____

e _____

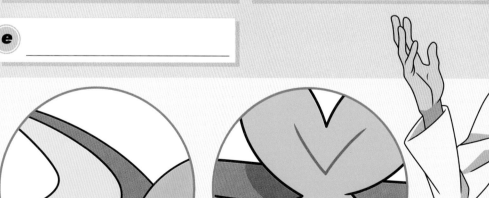

d   e

PARK PUZZLER

Which Pokémon are training in Cerise Park?
Solve the clues to find out.

1. Watch out for this Pokémon's Pyro Ball move!

`_ _ _ D _ _ _ _ E`

2. This Fossil Pokémon has a freezing upper body.

`_ R _ _ _ Z _ _ _`

3. This Pokémon drums to tap into its special power.

`_ _ L _ O _ _`

4. When scared, this Pokémon cries!

`_ _ _ _ L _`

5. These six individuals work together as one.

`_ A _ _ _ _ S`

COMPUTER ERROR!

Use the code to help you complete these scrambled Pokédex files.

🌢	🔥	🟤	🌸	🐌	⚡	🔷	🌿	⬭	⚡
C	D	E	L	N	P	R	S	T	W

1. `_ I _ I _ O B _ A`

2. `_ H _`   `_ A _ D`   `_ _ A K E`   `_ O K _ M O _`

3. `A`   `G _ O U _ D - _ Y _ _ _`

1. `_ H I _ V U _`

2. `_ H _`   `F O X`   `_ O K _ M O _`

3. `A`   `D A _ K - _ Y _ _`

ANSWERS ON PAGE 69

HOW TO DRAW SCORBUNNY

Warm up that pencil for some serious action!

JUST FOLLOW THE STEPS TO CREATE YOUR OWN LOYAL, FIERY POKÉMON.

YOU'LL NEED:

Pencil and paper | Eraser | Black pen | Colouring pens

1

With a pencil, draw the shapes below to guide you for Scorbunny's head and body.

2

Pencil in the outlines for its arms, legs and feet.

3

Outline its ears. They should match the length of its body (shoulders to feet) in size.

THE SPECIAL PADS ON ITS NOSE AND FEET RADIATE TREMENDOUS HEAT WHEN IT'S READY TO BATTLE. SCORBUNNY, GO!

44

Add circles for its eyes. Draw a rectangle between them.

Pencil in the nose, mouth and eye details.

Add the shapes to its collar and fluffy cheeks.

Complete the paw and foot lines.

Add the final details to the ears.

Draw over your outlines in black pen. Erase the guidelines, and then colour your Scorbunny!

GOTTA CATCH 'EM!

Solve the clues to identify which 10 awesome Pokémon you've caught in the Poké Balls!

1

A Fairy-type Pokémon that evolves from a Milcery and produces cream from its hands.

2

This fast-swimming Water-type Pokémon can spin its tail fins to leap from the water.

3

This Pokémon sends electricity through its speedy legs and can run for three full days.

4

A Flying- and Steel-type Pokémon that flies with ease even with heavy steel wings.

5

This clever Pokémon evolves from Sobble and battles using water balloons.

6

A Grass-type Pokémon that has special seeds filled with nutrients attached to its cotton head.

7

This Pokémon evolves from Snom and can cause blizzards with its huge chill-spreading wings.

8

A fully-evolved Psychic- and Fairy-type Pokémon that can blast opponents with a beam.

9

A Fire-type Rabbit Pokémon with thick, fluffy fur, who can juggle berries with its feet.

10

This Punk Pokémon evolves from Toxel and can keep its cool against any opponent.

Who got away? Unscramble the highlighted letters to reveal the Ground-type Pokémon who slipped away!

ANSWERS ON PAGE 69

47

POKÉ BALL PUZZLER

Battle your way to the centre of the Poké Ball by answering the questions below.

THE LAST LETTER OF EACH ANSWER IS THE FIRST LETTER OF THE NEXT!

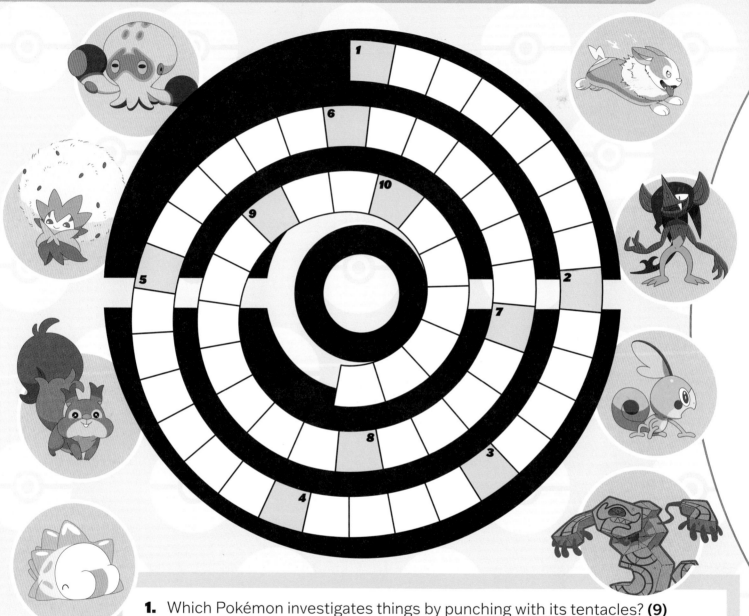

1. Which Pokémon investigates things by punching with its tentacles? **(9)**
2. Which Pokémon can bring all of its attackers to tears? **(6)**
3. Which Pokémon keeps its head iced all the time so it can stay cold? **(6)**
4. Which cotton-headed Pokémon spreads nutrients through its seeds? **(8)**
5. Which cheeky Pokémon is happiest when its cheeks are full of berries? **(7)**
6. Which Pokémon can beat a super-fast rhythm with its two sticks? **(8)**
7. Which sparky Pokémon is popular as a herding dog in the Galar region? **(6)**
8. Which Pokémon formed from a curse woven into an ancient painting? **(9)**
9. Which Pokémon can disguise itself as an icicle while it sleeps? **(4)**
10. Which Pokémon can stab opponents with its spear-like hair? **(7)**

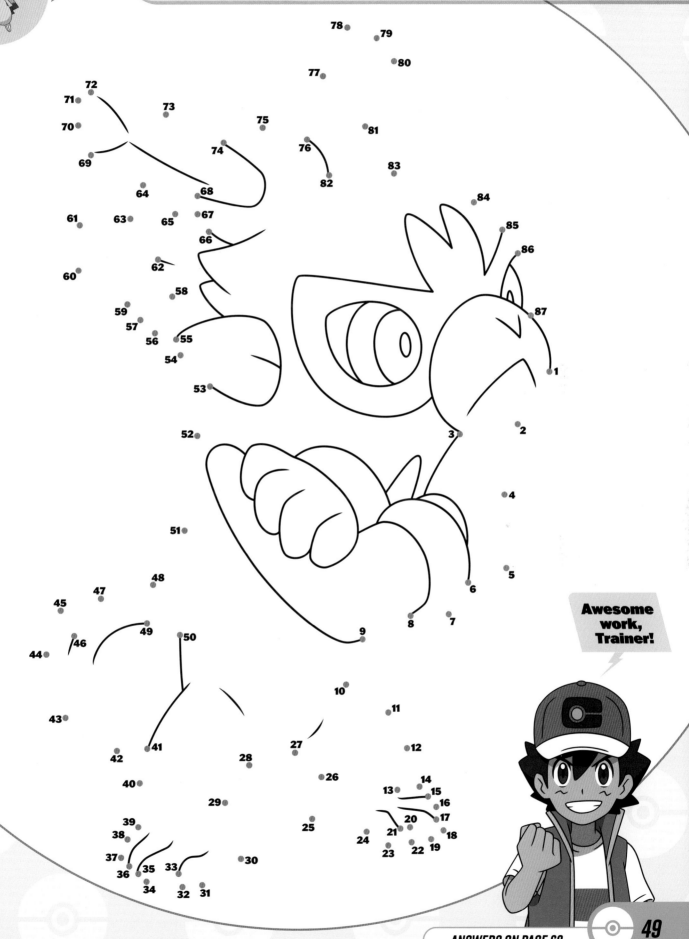

BRING YOUR ANSWER TO NUMBER 6 TO LIFE!
JOIN THE DOTS TO CATCH A DRUMMING POKÉMON BUDDY.

Awesome work, Trainer!

SEARCHING FOR CHIVALRY

STORY

It's time for Ash and Goh to take part in some intense training with their mighty Pokémon!

Goh and Ash were in Cerise Park, armed with leeks and practising their sword-fighting skills. Ash was determined to train hard and keep up with his Farfetch'd, who wanted to become a Leek Master. "Its leek techniques are getting sharper!" said Goh.
Ash agreed. "Ever since its loss to Gallade, it's been training day in and day out. And that's why I wanna help out in any way I can."

They had heard about a place called Castle of Chivalry, where trainers and Pokémon who wanted to find their true strength could complete challenges. Ash couldn't wait to go with Farfetch'd, and Goh decided to take Scyther, too.

When they arrived at The Castle of Chivalry, they were met by a mighty trainer dressed from head to toe in steel armour. "Ye who seek strength, I bid you Good Day!" the trainer proclaimed. "I am a member of the Kalos Elite Four. The Trainer of Steel, Wikstrom by name." He was accompanied by an Aegislash Pokémon.

"Now," said Wikstrom, "would you like to reach for the top together?" Everyone said they would, and Wikstrom was moved by their determination. "But why are we wearing the armour and not just the Pokémon?" Goh asked. "There is but one reason," answered Wikstrom, "and that is because you are trying to attain true strength! And once we begin our training, you will understand!"

Wikstrom explained there were three challenges to pass. The winners would receive The Knight Medal. The first trial was running ten laps around the castle, facing some challenges on the way. Everyone passed, but there wasn't much time to celebrate. It was time for the second trial! This one was called The Labyrinth of Doubt.

"A Pokémon and its Trainer must walk side by side, then emerge gloriously!" said Wikstrom. As soon as they entered the labyrinth, Ash and Goh were separated from each other by bars that came down from the ceiling. Now Ash and Farfetch'd, and Goh and Scyther, had to head in different directions.
"Let's meet up at the goal line!" called Ash.

Ash and Farfetch'd were finding a route through the maze when a cute Dedenne came out from a secret door in the wall. At first Ash thought it was sweet, but then Dedenne gave him an electric shock! He had been tricked. Ash fell to the ground, and when he looked up, Farfetch'd was already walking away.

"Hold on!" Ash called. "Wait for me!" But Farfetch'd was very determined. He kept walking until he reached a wall. Farfetch'd swung his leek and soon he had broken through the wall and opened up the path!

Wikstrom was watching everything over security cameras. "That Farfetch'd has a rare battle sense and attack power," Wikstrom said. "However, it will never attain true strength in its present state!"

Suddenly, Farfetch'd stepped on a trapdoor in the floor and fell through! Ash yelled and ran to the hole. The Pokémon was clinging to a ledge. Ash managed to pull Farfetch'd to safety, but the Pokémon dropped its leek! Ash threw himself into the hole to catch the leek, and then Farfetch'd jumped in to save Ash.

Ash handed the leek back to Farfetch'd. "Good thing it's still fine. You care about it more than anything, isn't that right?" Farfetch'd looked at his leek and back at Ash, thinking carefully. "Hmm, I think I see a change..." said Wikstrom, watching on his screen.

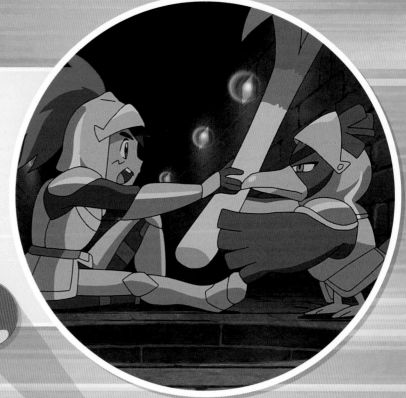

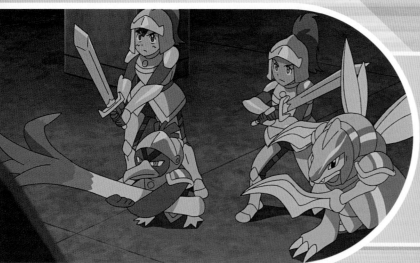

Just then, both Ash and Goh, and their Pokémon, broke through opposite walls and found themselves face-to-face. They had reached the finish! Wikstrom and Pikachu were there to greet them.

Next was the third and final trial. "If you are able to open the locked door behind us, you will pass the test," Wikstrom explained.
As he spoke, a Klefki appeared in front of them. They looked it up on the Rotom Phone: **Klefki. The Key Ring Pokémon. A Steel- and Fairy-type. Klefki draws in metal ions through the horn on its head. It loves collecting keys.**

"So, all we have to do is steal that key!" cried Ash. He and Goh set their Pokémon to work. But Aegislash defended Klefki.

At that moment, Goh and Ash jumped towards Klefki. But, Wikstrom leapt into their path with his sword drawn.
"These swords are harmless training replicas," said Wikstrom. "But you should never let down your guard!"
"This is why he had us wear armour!" Goh realised.
"Do you know what I think?" asked Ash.
"The training with the leeks is gonna pay off!"

Ash and Goh took it in turns to attack Wikstrom, but he dodged all of their attempts. "We can't let it end like this!" cried Ash, coming up with a plan.

"Okay, I'll deal with Wikstrom. Farfetch'd can you keep Aegislash busy? And while we're doing that, you and Scyther should go get the key."
"We got it!" called Goh.

They all charged. The startled Klefki quickly flew away as Goh and Scyther chased it. Ash and Wikstrom clashed swords with each other while Pikachu cheered on from the sidelines. Farfetch'd battled with Aegislash.

Wikstrom moved to strike Ash, but suddenly there was Farfetch'd, protecting his Trainer! Ash gasped and Wikstrom stood back. Aegislash tried to attack Farfetch'd, but Farfetch'd made a move of his own, and won. And just then, Goh and Scyther appeared, and they had the key! "Excellent!" said Wikstrom. Together, the team had passed the final trial.

Wikstrom presented them with their well-earned Knight Medals. "It is when you fight to protect those you hold dear that your strength increases many times!"

THE GANG DISCOVERED STRENGTH, BRAVERY AND KINDNESS BY THE WAY OF CHIVALRY. AND SO, WITH MANY ADVENTURES STILL TO COME, THE JOURNEY CONTINUES!

CATCH ADVENTURE RACE!

You've been entered into a Pokémon Adventure Race!

CAN YOU COMPLETE EACH PUZZLE TO CATCH A POKÉMON AND ZIP YOUR WAY ROUND THE COURSE?

START

CHALLENGE 1 — ODD SOBBLE OUT

One of these Pokémon is slightly different to the others. **Find it and circle it to catch it!**

1   2   3

4   5   6

CHALLENGE 2 — HIDE 'N' SEEK

A cunning Pokémon is staying out of sight! **Cross out the repeated letters, then unscramble the remaining five letters to catch it.**

X	A	H	I	J	B	E	G	K	M	O	P	F	Y	Q	R	L	X	D
D	F	T	G	M	Y	O	C	R	J	Q	H	V	E	L	A	N	P	B	V

_ _ I _ _

CHALLENGE 3 — POKÉ BALL, GO!

A little Pokémon is trying to throw you off your game!
Circle every third letter to find out who it is and catch them.

START YOUR COUNT HERE

Gotta get to the finish!

R C I A M M O R P L O I B B D I L A B M O O P R S

___ ___ ___ ___ ___ ___ ___ ___ ___ ___

CHALLENGE 4 — JIGSAW SCRAMBLE

Quick – it's the final challenge, Trainer!
Reorder these jigsaw pieces to catch a Galarian Linoone.

a   b   c   d   e

___ ___ ___ ___ ___

FINISH

Good job, Trainer!

ANSWERS ON PAGE 69

GIGANTAMAX NAME GAME

Ready, Trainer? It's a super-sized Pokémon name quiz! Complete the grid using the picture clues.

60

UH-OH, A CERTAIN POKÉMON IS CAUSING A STIR BACK AT CERISE PARK.

UNSCRAMBLE THE HIGHLIGHTED LETTERS IN THE GRID TO FIND OUT WHO IT IS!

EPIC EVOLUTIONS

Can you spot the Evolution sequences in the grid? **Circle them as you find them.**

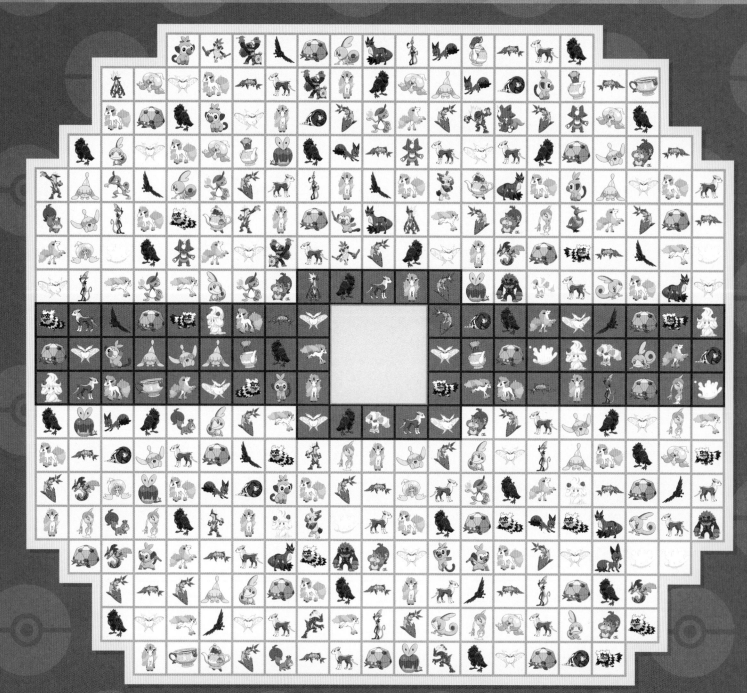

CAN YOU SPOT A POKÉMON IN THE GRID THAT _DOES NOT EVOLVE?_

ANSWERS ON PAGE 69

WHO'S YOUR FAVOURITE FULLY EVOLVED POKÉMON?

DRAW AND COLOUR IT HERE!

Way to go, Trainer!

MY NEW POKÉMON IS MEGA _____

ITS AWESOME ABILITY IS _____

 63

MAKE A DUGTRIO

Three heads are better than one! Follow the instructions below to make your own version of this awesome Mole Pokémon.

ASK AN ADULT TO HELP

YOU'LL NEED:

3 flat, oval stones • Black, white and pink paint • Fine paintbrush

Small plant pot • Soil • A handful of small pebbles

INSTRUCTIONS

1

Take your three oval stones – they will be the three heads of your Dugtrio. Paint black eyes with white dots, and a little pink nose, using the picture above to guide you.

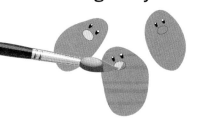

2

Fill your plant pot with soil and pat it down until you have a firm base.

3

Take your stones and place them in the pot, arranged in the trio shape.

4

Cover the soil surface around your stones with the small pebbles. Your Dugtrio is ready for action!

DID YOU KNOW?

The Dugtrio's three heads bob up and down to break up the surrounding soil so they can burrow through the ground extra fast!

POKéMON

ONLY IN GALAR!

CUT ALONG THE DOTTED LINE

LET'S DO BATTLE!

Which Fighting-type Pokémon would be your ultimate battle partner?

TRY THIS QUIZ TO FIND OUT!

START

Would you rather be Ash or Goh?

GOH →

Who would make a great partner – Grookey or Sobble?

GROOKEY

SOBBLE

ASH

Is the Galar region your favourite region?

YES →

What's more fun – training or catching Pokémon?

← **YES** ← Are you good at memorising Pokémon data?

CATCHING

NO

TRAINING

NO

Would you rather battle against a Bug- or Electric-type Pokémon?

Would you rather catch a Centiskorch or Silicobra?

SILICOBRA →

BUG

ELECTRIC

CENTISKORCH

Who would you pick for a battle with Team Rocket?

NO

Would you be an awesome researcher?

RILLABOOM

INTELEON

YES

GALARIAN FARFETCH'D

This brave warrior will swing his leek to victory!

FALINKS

Expect great teamwork with this awesome six-part Pokémon!

GRAPPLOCT

You can't beat the grip of this powerful Pokémon!

ANSWERS

Pikachu appears seven times, on pages 11, 15, 26, 29, 49, 61 and 67.

PAGES 8-9

Catch Some Pokémon!

The caught Pokémon are:

Carkol
Galarian Farfetch'd
Gossifleur
Galarian Linoone
Pincurchin

Scorbunny
Sizzlipede
Toxel
Cramorant

The Pokémon that evolves from Drizzile is Inteleon.

Goh's first partner was Scorbunny.

PAGES 10-11

Master Trainer Maze

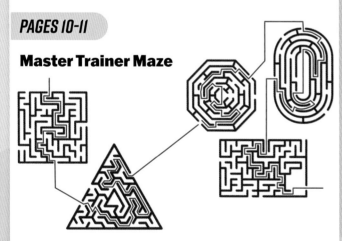

Eternatus is **b.** Poison and Dragon.

PAGES 12-13

Project Mew

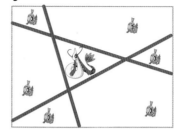

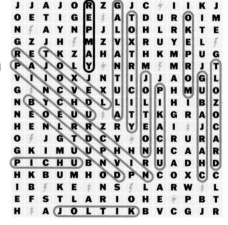

PAGE 14

The Hunt For Mew

PAGE 15

Electric Wordsearch

PAGE 25

Map Those Moves!

1. Falinks - **7B**
2. Galarian Rapidash - **11D**
3. Nickit - **2E**
4. Galarian Stunfisk - **20E**
5. Snorlax - **4E**
6. Wooloo - **10G**

PAGE 28

Fantastic Flyers

Braviary, Charizard, Rookidee, Corvisquire, Cramorant, Butterfree, Woobat, Hawlucha.

The Legendary Fire- and Flying-type Pokémon is Ho-Oh.

PAGES 42-43

Life in the Lab

UNDER THE MICROSCOPE: **a.** Yamper, **b.** Galarian Ponyta, **c.** Eiscue, **d.** Raichu, **e.** Grookey

PARK PUZZLER: **1.** Cinderace, **2.** Arctozolt, **3.** Rillaboom, **4.** Sobble, **5.** Falinks

COMPUTER ERROR!:
1. Silicobra
2. The Sand Snake Pokémon
3. A Ground-Type

1. Thievul
2. The Fox Pokémon
3. A Dark-Type

PAGES 46-47

Gotta Catch 'Em!

1. Alcremie, **2.** Barraskewda, **3.** Boltund, **4.** Corviknight, **5.** Drizzile, **6.** Eldegoss, **7.** Frosmoth, **8.** Hatterene, **9.** Raboot, **10.** Toxtricity

The Pokémon that got away is Sandaconda.

PAGES 48-49

Poké Ball Puzzler
1. Clobbopus, **2.** Sobble, **3.** Eiscue, **4.** Eldegoss, **5.** Skwovet, **6.** Thwackey, **7.** Yamper, **8.** Runerigus, **9.** Snom, **10.** Morgrem

PAGES 58-59

Catch Adventure Race!

CHALLENGE 1: Sobble 5

CHALLENGE 2: NICKIT

CHALLENGE 3: IMPIDIMP

CHALLENGE 4: e,d,b,a,c

PAGES 60-61

Gigantamax Name Game

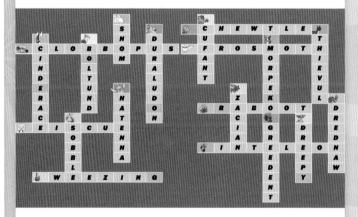

The Pokémon causing a stir is Grookey.

PAGES 62-63

Epic Evolutions

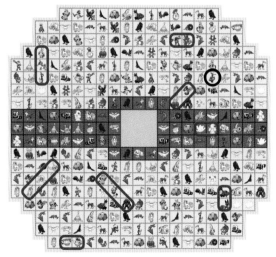

The Pokémon in the grid that does not evolve is Cramorant.